CONTENTS

STOP!

A POEM TO SHARE

WRITTEN BY ALISON CONDON
ILLUSTRATED BY MARTIN BAILEY

"Stop!" says
the red light.
"You must not go!"

"Slow down!" says
the orange light.
"You must go slow!"

"Go," says
the green light.
"Go, go, go!
The traffic can go
while I say so."

Red light,
orange light,
green light, too.
They all tell the
traffic what to do!

STOP AND GO!

Written by Edwin Johns
Illustrated by Helen Humphries

"Look and learn,"
said Grandma.

"Stop!" said Ben.

"Go!" said Sally.

"Look and learn,"
said Grandpa.

"Stop!" said Ben.

"Go!" said Sally.

"Look and learn,"
said Dad.

"Stop!" said Ben.

"Go!" said Sally.

"Look and learn," said Mum.

"Stop!" said Dad.

"Go!" said Ben
and Sally.

Who Stopped the Traffic?

WRITTEN BY MARIE GIBSON
ILLUSTRATED BY MARTIN BAILEY

21

Elephant went
to cross the road,
but a big, red
bus came by.

Tiger went
to cross the road,
but a little, blue
car came by.

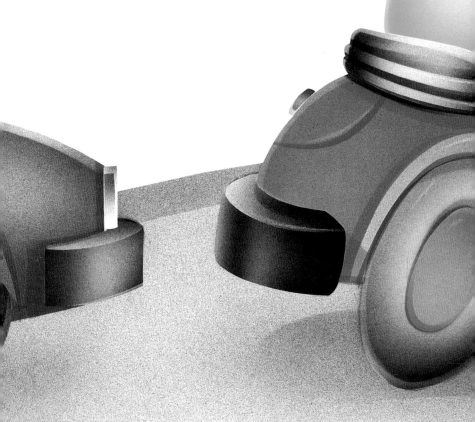

Turtle went
to cross the road,
but a big, green
truck came by.

"How can we
cross the road?"
they said.
"The traffic
is too fast."

Then Zebra said,
"Cross over here.
I will stop them
from going past!"

32